EVALINE THEO

RESILIENCE PARENTING

The Essential Guide to Resilient and Mindful
Parenting, Learn Tips and Advice on How to Become
a Better Parent to Your Kids

Descrierea CIP a Bibliotecii Naţionale a României
EVALINE THEO
    RESILIENCE PARENTING. The Essential Guide to Resilient and Mindful Parenting, Learn Tips and Advice on How to Become a Better Parent to Your Kids / Evaline Theo – Bucharest: Editura My Ebook, 2021
    ISBN

EVALINE THEO

RESILIENCE PARENTING

The Essential Guide to Resilient and Mindful Parenting, Learn Tips and Advice on How to Become a Better Parent to Your Kids

My Ebook Publishing House
Bucharest, 2021

TABLE OF CONTENTS

CHAPTER 1

ACTIVE LISTENING TO YOUR CHILD

Communicating with our children can be a difficult task at times. We feel like they're not listening to us; they feel like we're not listening to them. Good listening and communication skills are essential to successful parenting. Your child's feelings, views and opinions have worth, and you should make sure you take the time to sit down and listen openly and discuss them honestly.

It seems to be a natural tendency to react rather than to respond. We pass judgment based on our own feelings and experiences. However, responding means being receptive to our child's feelings and emotions, and allowing them to express themselves openly and honestly without fear of repercussion from us. By reacting, we send our child the message that their feelings and opinions are invalid. But responding and asking questions about why the child feels that way opens a dialog that allows them to discuss their feelings further, and allows you a better understanding of where they're coming from.

Responding also gives you an opportunity to work out a solution or a plan of action with your child that perhaps they would not have come up with on their own. Your child will also appreciate the fact that maybe you do indeed understand how they feel.

It's crucial in these situations to give your child your full and undivided attention. Put down your newspaper, stop doing dishes, or turn off the television so you can hear the full situation and make eye contact with your child. Keep calm, be inquisitive, and afterwards offer potential solutions to the problem.

Don't discourage your child from feeling upset, angry, or frustrated. Our initial instinct may be to say or do something to steer our child away from it, but this can be a detrimental tactic. Again, listen to your child, ask questions to find out why they are feeling that way, and then offer potential solutions to alleviate the bad feeling.

Just as we do, our children have feelings and experience difficult situations. Actively listening and participating with our child as they talk about it demonstrates to them that we do care, we want to help and we have similar experiences of our own that they can draw from. Remember, respond - don't react.

CHAPTER 2

CELEBRATE YOUR CHILD'S UNIQUENESS

Just like a snowflake or a fingerprint, every child is unique in their own special way. Every child has a unique way of feeling, thinking, and interacting with others. Some children are shy, while others are outgoing; some are active, while others are calm; some are fretful, while others are easy-going. As a loving and nurturing parent, it's your job to encourage them to embrace their uniqueness and celebrate their individual qualities.

Allow your child to express themselves through their interests. They may find a creative outlet in theatre, dancing or art, or they may be exceptionally talented in the sciences. Encourage them to embrace what they like to do, what interests them, and what makes them happy. Help them realize that they don't need to worry about being 'like everyone else.'

Teach your child to make positive choices, and praise them for good deeds, behaviors and positive traits they possess. Encourage them to become actively involved in their community, and introduce them to activities that promote a sense of cooperation and accomplishment. Be firm, yet fair, when handing down discipline for misdeeds or misbehaviors, and make certain the rules and consequences for breaking the rules are clearly defined. Show a cooperative, loving and united front with your spouse when it comes to discipline.

Accept and celebrate your child's uniqueness. Remember that your child is an individual. Allow your child to have his or her own personal preferences and feelings, which may be different from your own.

And finally, encourage your child to be true to themselves by doing the same. Show your child how to make positive choices with the choices you make, and that nobody is perfect and you too make mistakes. Show your child that mistakes can be a great learning experience, and that they should not be ashamed or embarrassed about making them.

CHAPTER 3

CONNECT WITH YOUR CHILD,
BUT DON'T OVERDO IT

We all want to connect and be involved with our child. Children of involved parents generally feel more confident, assured, and have a higher level of self-esteem. They excel in school and do well in extracurricular activities and with their hobbies.

But is there such a thing as too much involvement? It's imperative when you're becoming involved with your school-aged child's activities and academics that you recognize the line of what being too involved can be.

Remember, you're becoming involved in your child's life. It's important that you don't intrude too much upon it. Children need their space and privacy and they need to be able to develop their own skills, talents and abilities. In our eagerness to help our child succeed, it's tempting to step in and start doing things for them because you feel they are doing them incorrectly or inadequately. But remember, you had to learn too, and this is their chance to learn on their own.

Be there to encourage and support your child, and offer praise at a job well done. But also remember to step back and allow your child to learn from their own mistakes, and to develop their own way of doing things. We all know from our own life experiences that there's always more than just one way to do something, and just because your child is doing it differently than you would doesn't make it wrong. Who knows, it could present a terrific opportunity for you to learn from your child as well.

In addition, try not to become too overbearing or nosy when it comes to their social life. Be available for them should they need to talk and encourage them to share their troubles with you so you can help them sort through a problem. But if they say they don't want to talk about it or they just need some time to figure things out for themselves, respect that need by letting them know you're available whenever they need you. This is an important part of growing up, and allowing a child to figure his or her own way through things is an integral part of that process.

CHAPTER 4

CONTROL YOUR ANGER,
DON'T LET IT CONTROL YOU

Anger can be a paralyzing and debilitating condition. But it can be a terrifying and degrading experience for your child if you're taking your anger out on them. Physical and verbal abuse of a child can have lasting and lethal implications, so it's crucial that as a parent, you do whatever is necessary to keep your anger in check.

As a parent, you have a wonderful opportunity to undo the wrongs that were done to you as a child, if you had an angry and abusive parent or parents. Parenting can be very curative, it can demonstrate to you where your troubles lie, and it can inspire you to fix them. Perhaps your past is filled with unresolved hurt and anger. If so, take the necessary steps to heal yourself. If you don't, you could unwillingly and unthinkingly harm your child.

Studies have shown that children whose mothers often expresses anger are more likely to be difficult to discipline. Identify problems from your past and honestly look at current situations that are angering you. Maybe you aren't fulfilled at work; perhaps you and your spouse are having relationship troubles, or maybe you have other personal issues or unfulfilled goals that are bothering you. If all your child ever sees is your angry face and hears an angry voice, that's what they'll most likely grow into as well.

It's important to 'pick your battles' when parenting. Accidents and nuisances don't warrant the energy and agony it takes to get angry. But misbehaviors such as a child hurting themselves, others or property demand a firm, quick and appropriate response from you. You will probably have to continually remind yourself that the small stuff isn't worth getting worked up over. And remind yourself also that you're the one in control of your anger; don't let your anger control you. Put yourself in time out, take a deep breath, walk away, and do whatever you have to in order to get a grip on yourself before addressing the situation, if you feel your anger coming on strong.

CHAPTER 5

DO AS I SAY AND A I DO

Children learn to imitate at a very young age. It's how they learn to behave, care for themselves, develop new skills, and communicate with others. From their earliest moments they watch you closely and pattern their own behavior and beliefs after yours. Your examples become permanent images, which will shape their attitudes and actions for the rest of their life.

It's important to be responsible, consistent and loving with your child. This also holds true for the relationship you have with your spouse, your parents, and other family members and friends that are also a part of your child's life. Own up to mistakes when you make them, and communicate openly and honestly with all family members.

It's also important to take good care of yourself. When we're focusing on what's best for our child, it's easy to neglect our own needs. Your child and your family are counting on you physically and emotionally, so it's imperative that you teach your child by example that taking care of yourself helps you to take care of them and the rest of your family. This shows your child that not only do you love them and the rest of the family, but you love yourself as well. This is an important step in teaching your child about self esteem. It may involve getting a sitter and treating yourself out to dinner and a movie, or doing another favorite activity on your own. This teaches your child that you are not only their parent, but your own person with your own interests and needs, and also gives them a chance to show you how well they can do without you with them for a while.

It's also important to nurture your relationship with your spouse. Let your child see that you communicate in a positive and healthy manner with one another, and show love and affection for one another, so your child can begin to learn early on what a healthy marriage should be like.

You'll soon see your child patterning many of his or her behaviors after your own. So make sure that what you say and do around your child will help build a strong sense of security and self esteem.

CHAPTER 6

ENCOURAGING PLAY ENCOURAGES
A CHILD'S DEVELOPMENT

We've all heard the phrase, "Oh, that's child's play." It implies that something is easy, frivolous and unimportant in the overall scheme of things. But to a child, child's play is essential to their mental, social, emotional, and physical development.

We all know that children like to play. But what we may not know is the importance of play in a child's life. Play is essential to every area of a child's growth and development.

Play provides a means for energy to be put to use. It strengthens and refines small and large motor skills, and it builds stamina and strength. Sensory learning develops mostly through play. Play is significant to physical development in that without it, the body could not grow and develop normally.

Children possess a natural curiosity. They explore, learn, and make sense out of their environment by playing. Parents and educators alike can support this learning activity by ensuring age-appropriate toys, materials and environments are available to the child.

Play enables children to know things about the world and to discover information essential to learning. Through play, children learn basic concepts such as colors, counting, how to build things, and how to solve problems. Thinking and reasoning skills are at work every time a child engages in some type of play.

Children learn to relate to one another, negotiate roles, share, and obey rules through play. They also learn how to belong to a group and how to be part of a team. A child obtains and retains friends through play.

Play fulfills many needs including a sense of accomplishment, successfully giving and receiving attention, and the need for self-esteem. It helps them develop a strong sense of self, and is emotionally satisfying to them. They learn about fairness, and through pretending, learn appropriate ways of expressing emotion such as anger, fear, frustration, and stress, and discover ways of dealing with these feelings.

So encourage your child's play. Color pictures, make finger paintings, build buildings and imaginary cities with blocks, and build a tent in the middle of the living room to go camping! And as we all know, childhood is fleeting, so let them enjoy being a kid while they are one!

CHAPTER 7

EXPECT ONLY THE BEST
FROM YOUR CHILD

Expect the best from your child. If you expect the best behavior and performance from your child, it's often what you will get. Children pick up on our beliefs about them, form a self-concept that matches that belief, and perform accordingly. If we expect them to be lazy, they'll be lazy, which will confirm our expectations for them, and the cycle toward failure is started. If, on the other hand, we expect our kids to be successful, productive, creative, and responsible, and honestly believe it to be true, then our children can't help but rise to the occasion and confirm our best opinions of them with their positive actions. So expect nothing but the best from your children and watch them fulfill your expectations.

Praise your child often when they perform a good deed or accomplish a new task. Set simple, clear and consistent rules so your child knows exactly what is expected and the consequences of misbehaving or breaking the rules. Maintain a consistent daily routine for your child as much as possible, and make sure your child gets lots of physical activity and time to play and socialize with their friends. Encourage your child to learn how to make appropriate choices, and encourage your child to do things for themselves.

Allow your child to talk about strong feelings, which will help them work through their anger and frustration.

Above all, be a positive role model for your child, as their strongest educator is your example. Take care of yourself, and expect the best from yourself. Make appropriate choices and be firm, yet fair, when disciplining your child. Make sure to spend lots of quality time with your child, and encourage them to become involved in activities that foster cooperation and a sense of accomplishment. If you have great expectations of your child, you'll be greatly pleased in the end.

CHAPTER 8

GET INVOLVED IN YOUR CHILD'S ACTIVITIES, HOBBIES AND SCHOOL

It's probably no secret that children who have involved parents are more happy, healthy, and well- adjusted, and excel at their educational and extracurricular pursuits. It can increase their cognitive development, keep them motivated, strengthen the parent-child relationship, and have a direct positive influence on their overall academic achievement. In turn, it can also help parents achieve a positive outlook on their parenting, increase their own self confidence and self-esteem, and most likely feel more satisfied with their child's educational experience at school.

But where do you get involved? With today's busy schedules between home, work, and school, it may feel like the average family has very little quality time to offer. However, different options and levels of commitment are available to fit every parent's availability, and with some careful planning and dedication, you can make it a positive experience for both yourself and your child.

First of all, discover what your child is most passionate about. Maybe you've thought about volunteering for the school bake sale to raise money, but your child is actually more actively involved in her local Girl Scouts troop. If that's the case, then get together with the other Girl Scout parents and see what you can contribute to help the troop. Maybe you could organize a bake sale to benefit their next summer outing.

It's also important to consider what skills, talents and abilities you can bring to the table. Maybe your child's school is in desperate need of your help organizing a fundraiser, but your skills in sewing and designing might better serve the school if you were to help make the costumes for the school play.

Remember, you want this to be a positive experience for both of you, and if your child senses that you're not happy with what you've chosen to become involved in, then they likely will not be happy either.

But the bottom line is to get involved and stay involved. Children of involved parents are less likely to get into mischief, have emotional problems, or have trouble in school. You benefit by connecting with and staying connected to your child. It's a win-win situation for you both.

CHAPTER 9

LEARN FROM YOUR MISTAKES
AND SO WILL YOUR CHILD

Everyone makes mistakes. Granted, some mistakes are more significant than others and harder to get over, but they are a part of life. How individuals deal with those mistakes is significant to their self- esteem. Children who are taught from an early age to admit to their mistakes understand that it's not a crime to make one, and they seem to have the ability to cope much better with them. They recognize that a mistake was made and admit the error. Most importantly, these children also develop a strategy to change the mistake and not do the same thing again.

The process of making and learning from mistakes is an extremely valuable life skill for everyone, because learning involves risks. Children don't succeed every time they take a risk, but they try something new and most likely learn from it as a result.

Children with low self-esteem deal with making a mistake quite differently. More often than not, these children use the experience to devalue themselves. Instead of looking at the error as an opportunity to learn, these children interpret the experience as a reason to quit and never try again. They view it as a devaluing and humiliating experience.

You can help your child cope with mistakes by first making sure they understand that everyone makes mistakes, even you. Own up to your own mistakes to teach them there's no shame in making them. Make sure they understand that it's okay to make mistakes. This presents a great opportunity to tell your child what you've learned to do differently the next time. Then, offer strategies to turn mistakes into learning opportunities. In the process, you can provide your child with an opportunity to enhance their self-esteem and accept responsibility for the mistakes they make. Help your child to realize that the mistake is the problem, and not them. Then help them develop a positive plan for the next time around, and what they'll do differently the next time to avoid making the same mistake again.

CHAPTER 10

MAKE QUALITY TIME
WITH YOUR CHILD COUNT

In today's busy world, work, household chores and social activities all put a strain on your time with your child. But as you well know, it's imperative that you spend quality time together. It helps strengthen the bond between parent and child, and lets your child know you can be trusted and counted on. Children who spend quality time with their parents often do better in school, and excel in extracurricular activities, hobbies or sports. And though it can be 'scheduled' to a degree, it's something that happens when you least expect it. Therefore, it's important that you do spend as much time as possible with your child in a relaxed atmosphere and do things together that you both enjoy.

But you're asking yourself, "Where am I going to find the time? My schedule's crazy enough as it is!" Well, for something as important as your child, you need to start digging around in that crazy schedule and find the time. Prioritizing is the key.

Here are some helpful suggestions on how to make the most of your time and find quality time where you least expect it:

Look at your household chore list and decide which ones can be left undone or be done imperfectly in order to make more family time. You might also want to consider leaving certain things until after your child has gone to bed to make the most of your time together.

Make some of your everyday routines together count. Sing some favorite silly songs on the way to daycare, or use that drive to and from school as a great opportunity to discuss what's happening in your child's life.

If you have more than one child, realize that each of them needs your individual attention. You may really have to juggle things around to make this happen, but try to be flexible and creative when spending time with each of your kids. And no matter what, don't skip those individual times with each child.

When you do that, you show them they're lower down on the priority list than the dry cleaning or the grocery shopping.

Children thrive on stability and routines, so plan your quality times so that they can take place regularly. Maybe you can walk the dog together on weekend mornings, take a shopping excursion together, have a scheduled night each week for a sit-down dinner together, or make a trip to the park.

CHAPTER 11

TEACH YOUR CHILD TO GIVE RESPECT, AND THEY'LL GAIN RESPECT IN RETURN

One of the most important things you can teach your child is respect, and the best way to teach respect is to show respect. When a child experiences respect, they know what it feels like and begin to understand how important it is.

Keep in mind the saying, "Do unto others as you would have them do unto you."

Respect is an attitude. Being respectful helps a child succeed in life. If children don't have respect for peers, authority, or themselves, it's almost impossible for them to succeed. A respectful child takes care of belongings and responsibilities, and a respectful child gets along with peers.

Schools teach children about respect, but parents have the most influence on how respectful children become. Until children show respect at home, it's unlikely they will show it anywhere else.

How can you show respect to your child? If you do something wrong, admit it and apologize. Don't embarrass, insult or make fun of your child. Compliment them and let your child make choices and take responsibility. Listen to your child's side of the story before making a decision on an issue or problem. Be polite and use "please" and "thank you" when asking them to do things. Knock before entering your child's room. Keep promises. Show your child that you mean what you say. And give your child your full attention.

And most importantly, teach your children that respect is earned. Make sure that you are leading by example and modelling respectful behavior. Be a law-abiding citizen. Show concern for your environment, animals and other people. Openly and honestly discuss examples of witnessed disrespect.

In addition, teach your child to respect themselves. Self-respect is one of the most important forms of respect. Once we respect ourselves, it is easier to respect others.

Help them set and achieve goals. Encourage honesty and teach them that people make mistakes, and that they are the best way to learn.

Most importantly, praise your child often for good deeds, behaviors or traits, and tell them you love them at least several times each day. You're sure to raise a child capable of giving and gaining respect.

CHAPTER 12

TEACH CHILDREN TO RESPECT
BY TREATING THEM WITH RESPECT

In order to teach a child to treat others with respect and dignity, they must also be treated that way, and childhood is a time for children to learn about the world, including how to get along with others. Parents play an essential role in teaching children how to form healthy relationships and grow into socially adept individuals. This social competence allows children to be cooperative and generous, express their feelings, and empathize with others.

The most effective way to teach children this lesson is by modelling the behavior you want to encourage. Every time you say "please" or lend a helping hand, you are showing your children how you would like them to act. Ask for your children's help with daily tasks, and accept their offers of help. Praise your child's good behavior and traits often, and help them realize how good it feels inside to do a good deed or be generous with another person.

Socially competent children are ones who have a strong sense of self-worth and importance. When a child feels good about themselves, it's easy for them to treat others in a positive, helpful manner.

Encourage acts of generosity through sharing and cooperation. Let your child know when it's someone else's turn with a toy or on the swing and praise their ability to recognize this on their own. Thank them for being polite and respectful and for sharing and cooperating.

Children know from their own experiences that words can hurt, and that name-calling, teasing, or excluding others affects how people feel. Children want to be treated fairly, but they don't always understand how to treat others the same way. One way to teach fairness is to explain a rule to your child, pointing out that it applies to him or her as well as to others.

CHAPTER 13

SUCCESSFUL TWO-WAY COMMUNICATIONS WITH YOUR CHILD

One of the most frustrating challenges we face as parents is communicating effectively with our child. Though we strive to open an honest two-way line of communication with our child, we become frustrated when it appears as though their attention isn't solely on us or the conversation at hand. Yet we seem to find it's perfectly acceptable to discuss things with them while reading the paper, folding clothes, or working on the computer, and then are often left wondering when the lines of communication broke.

Children are by nature easily distracted and not always responsive to their environment. It is the responsibility of the parent to emphasize positive patterns of communication and ensure the child learns that ignoring communication is not acceptable. Early prevention, in the form of educating your child about the proper forms of communication, is the key to ensuring that the non-verbal agreement does not take hold. Teach your child by example. Remain completely and totally focused on them and the conversation at hand. Turn off the television, allow calls to go to the voicemail, or go into a room where there are no distractions.

Talk to your child, and explain to them in age-appropriate terms how they are communicating and why their method doesn't work. Show your child how to communicate effectively, even when the questions are hard.

Make yourself an active listener. Let them voice their opinion or side of the story and ask questions to ensure you understand their viewpoint.

Be constant in the manner in which you communicate with you child. Send the same message with each and every interaction. Allow your child to see that you will call their attention to those times that the unwanted behavior rears its ugly head.

Kids will be kids, and they will sometimes be distracted and non-communicative. You are the expert in knowing your child's behavior and can best judge the improvement in their communications. The best way to ensure healthy communication patterns is to model positive communication skills.

CHAPTER 14

THE DETRIMENTAL EFFECTS OF VERBAL ABUSE
AND HOW TO STOP THE CYCLE

"Sticks and stones may break my bones, but names will never hurt me."

That's just not true. Name-calling hurts - especially when the person doing it is a parent, a teacher, or a coach. Yelling and screaming might have been the way you were brought up, and you might think it worked for you, so why wouldn't it work for your kids? But did it? Remember how it made you feel. You probably felt belittled, devalued, and insignificant. You certainly don't want your own children to feel that way. It may cause emotional trauma that can result in long-term hurt. Among other things, verbal abuse can undermine your child's self-esteem, damage his or her ability to trust and form relationships, and chip away at his or her academic and social skills. Name-calling, swearing, insulting, threatening bodily harm, blaming or using sarcasm are all forms of verbal abuse.

What are the signs that a child is suffering from verbal abuse? They may have a very negative self-image. They may commit acts that are self-destructive, such as cutting, hitting or scratching themselves, as well as other reckless and dangerous activities. They may exhibit physical aggression, be delinquent in school, or display interpersonal problems. They may hit other children, frequently fight with classmates at school, or be cruel to animals. They may also exhibit delays in their social, physical, academic or emotional development.

Recent research suggests that children who suffer from verbal abuse are highly likely to become victims of abuse later in life, become abusive themselves, or become depressed and self-destructive later in life

It's normal for most parents, at one time or another, to feel frustrated and angry with their children. They may lash out verbally in these instances and say things they later regret. It's when these instances become more and more frequent that there is cause for concern. If this describes you, it's imperative that you seek professional help to learn more positive, meaningful and constructive forms of discipline, and for help in learning methods to control your anger. Remember to give yourself a time out if you feel an outburst coming on. Try to refrain from saying mean, sarcastic or belittling things to your child. Remember, your child learns what he or she lives. Don't be a bad example and teach him or her bad behavior early on.

Remember that your child is a precious gift and should be treated with love, kindness, respect and tenderness. If you exhibit these to your child on a daily basis, they will learn what they live and grow to do the same as adults.

CHAPTER 15

OUR EVER-CHANGING ROLE AS A PARENT

We watch our children grow right before our very eyes. It seems like yesterday they were a baby learning to crawl, walk, and feed themselves, and now they're in school, involved in activities, making friends, and learning to be more and more independent. Parents before us have said that from the time they're born, we are constantly learning to let go. As a result, our parenting strategies have to change. As our child grows, develops, learns, and matures, so does our parenting role.

As your child has grown, you undoubtedly have discovered that they have their own unique personality and temperament. You've probably unconsciously redeveloped your parenting skills around the individual needs of your child. And no two children are exactly alike, and therefore, your parenting style shouldn't be either. Some children may need more guidance and feel more unsure of themselves, so we've become used to having to guide, lead, show and encourage that child consistently through their childhood while still trying to encourage independence and give praise in order to build their self esteem and confidence level. Yet another child may be very intrinsically motivated and very willful and not need a great deal of guidance or leadership from you. While you encourage their independence, it's also important that you also encourage their ability to ask for help when needed and continue to praise good deeds, actions, and traits.

The most important tools we have in order to successfully adjust our parenting skills are our eyes and our ears. We have to see what's going on with our child and we have to hear what they are telling us. It's important that we encourage our child to be their own individual, while still being available to them at whatever level or degree they need us to be. Sometimes it's situation-specific as well. A child may not need us to be as directly involved with their schooling to ensure their overall academic success, but they may need us to be more involved in their social life as they may be feeling a bit shaky or scared when it comes to making new friends or meeting new people.

So the bottom line is this: as your child grows and changes, so should your parenting skills. Keep your eyes and ears open and communicate honestly and openly with your child, and you'll both mature gracefully.

Printed by Libri Plureos GmbH in Hamburg, Germany